Fatima Family Apostolate & CCC of America

Fatima Educational Program

Book and Film Project for Children

THE COMPANION LESSON BOOK TO THE CLASSIC ANIMATED FILM
THE DAY THE SUN DANCED, THE TRUE STORY OF FATIMA

The Miracle of the Dancing Sun at Fatima
Messages from Mary

This book was inspired by the lifelong work of Father Robert J. Fox who is the founder of the Fatima Family Apostolate International and the Cadet's Program. Father Fox also wrote the script for the animated film, *The Day the Sun Danced, The True Story of Fatima.*

By

John Preiss
Michael La Corte
Karla Alfaro

Illustrators

Becca Klein
Mari Jo Bueno

Graphic Designer

Kathy Yoder

Cover Art by

Marisa Antonello
Victoria Laidley

**Presented through a collaboration of the
Fatima Family Apostolate International, Inc. and CCC of America, Inc.**

This is an advance reading copy not for sale.
After you have read this book we would love to hear what you think.
Please contact us by email at johncpreiss@fatimafamily.org

Published by:

Fatima Family Apostolate International, Inc.
PO Box 269
Hanceville, AL 35077

800-213-5541

www.FatimaFamily.org
johncpreiss@fatimafamily.org

DEDICATION

This book is dedicated to
Father Robert J. Fox

A Life of Service to God and Founder of
The Fatima Family Apostolate International

The Fatima Family Apostolate International and CCC of America dedicate this book to Our Heavenly Mother, Father Robert J. Fox and the children of the world.

Our Lady of Fatima delivered a powerful message of Hope, and Father Fox dedicated his 50 years as a priest to sharing this message to a world in need. Twenty years ago Father Fox wrote the story for the award-winning classic animated film, "The Day the Sun Danced, the True Story of Fatima," produced by CCC of America. This timeless film helps many thousands of children develop Catholic values that guide them throughout their lives.

"The Miracle of the Dancing Sun at Fatima, Messages from Mary" is a beautiful companion learning book to the animated film and a testament to the powerful partnering of two organizations with a shared mission. We pray that children in every country will have the opportunity to learn from this book and the companion film. We also wish to provide these faith-building materials to parishes, religious schools and their students in all countries.

The publication of this book marks the re-launch of the Cadets 4 Mary program started by Father Fox almost 40 years ago. Through the decades millions of Cadets made a personal commitment to Our Blessed Mother to pray daily and to live the message of Fatima. The "Cadets 4 Mary" program cultivates virtues that last a lifetime. For further information see page 42.

PRAYER FOR THEIR CANONIZATION

Most Holy Trinity, Father, Son and Holy Spirit, I adore You profoundly and I thank You for the Apparitions of the Most Holy Virgin in Fatima.

By the infinite merits of the Sacred Heart of Jesus and through the intercession of the Immaculate Heart of Mary I implore You – if it should be for Your greater glory and the good of our souls – to glorify in the sight of Your Holy Church Blessed Francisco, Jacinta and Sister Lucia, granting us through their intercession the grace which we implore. AMEN.

ĬV₀

THE MIRACLE OF THE
DANCING SUN
AT FATIMA
"Messages from Mary"

Table of Contents

Our Story Begins

Our story begins on a lovely spring day in 1916. It is the true story about three children and a very important message they received from Heaven that is meant to be shared with your family and friends.

Why don't we follow them and see what happens?

The three children lived in Fatima, Portugal. Francisco Marto was 8 and his sister Jacinta was 6 and their cousin Lucia dos Santos was 9.

Their village is made of houses built of stucco with red tile roofs and cobblestone streets.

Do you see the sheep? That means they live in a farming community. While taking care of sheep the children play games, sing songs, and spend some time praying.

Lucia is leading the others on this beautiful spring day filled with the fresh smell of flowers in the crisp clean air. "Hurry up," says Lucia. **"We can play but, first we must pray."**

The Hail Mary Prayer

Hail Mary, full of grace, the Lord is with you;

blessed are you among women,

and blessed is the fruit of your womb, Jesus.

Holy Mary, Mother of God,

pray for us sinners

now and at the hour of our death.

Amen.

PORTUGAL Fatima

here is Fatima?

Lisbon

As we shall see, the Hail Mary Prayer is a very important prayer. It is important to understand what the prayer means and where it comes from.

The first line comes from the Bible when the Angel Gabriel asked our Blessed Mother if she would be Jesus's mother.

What are the first five words in the first line of the Hail Mary prayer?

— — — —   — — — — —   — — — — —   — —   — — — — —

I will offer a Hail Mary prayer for: (please check the boxes below)

☐ My family   ☐ Children around the world

☐ Our Pope   ☐ _____ (fill in the blank)

  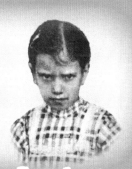

Francisco Lucia Jacinta
This is a picture of the three shepherd children.

Do they look unhappy?

The children were very happy and played often.
They look frightened in their picture becuase back then
a very bright and scary flash of light was needed to take a picture.

3

First Visit of the Angel

On a lovely spring day in 1916, a very unusual thing happened. Suddenly, the three children saw a bright light over the trees that came toward them. A beautiful Angel appeared and said, "Do not be afraid! I am the Angel of Peace. Pray with me."

The Angel immediately knelt down, bowed his forehead to the ground and prayed the Pardon Prayer three times.

The Angel said "Pray this way. The Hearts of Jesus and Mary are ready to hear you." When the Angel left, the children prayed, they felt even more love for God and they felt God's great love for them.

? What is Hope?

Hope comes from God. In good times and in times of pain or difficulty, we always have hope because we believe in God, we adore God, we love God and God is always with us.

Fill in the blank with the matching letters from the Pardon Prayer:

B __ __ __ __ __ __ in God

A __ __ __ __ God

H __ __ __ and

L __ __ __ God

The Pardon Prayer

My God, I believe, I adore,
I hope, and I love You.

I beg pardon for those who do
not believe, do not adore,
do not hope, and do
not love You.

Second Visit of the Angel

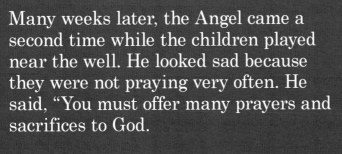

Many weeks later, the Angel came a second time while the children played near the well. He looked sad because they were not praying very often. He said, "You must offer many prayers and sacrifices to God.

With these words the Angel disappeared and the children spent hours praying the Pardon Prayer the Angel taught them.

❓ What is a Sacrifice?

A sacrifice is giving up something important to you and offering it to God. God does not want us to do anything that is harmful to ourselves or others but He does want us to help others. Later in this story we will learn how the three children sacrificed so much to please God and help others.

You can offer your time to God and use it to:

- help someone
- pray
- do a good deed

Billy was not feeling well and of course it was important for him to tell his parents. While he was feeling bad he said to God, "God, as long as I have these bad feelings, I offer them to help fix the pain sin causes." God was pleased and Billy felt better because he was able to turn his pain into something good until it went away.

Susan wanted to watch TV but instead she decided to help her younger brother Luke learn his prayers. She knew this was a big sacrifice for her but it made her happy when she asked God to use her sacrifice to bring peace to those in need.

What sacrifices can you offer God this week?

1. _____

2. _____

3. _____

Third Visit of the Angel

The third and last time the Angel appeared to the children, he brought them the most precious gift of all; the Holy Eucharist. The Angel held a Host in one hand and a beautiful golden Chalice in the other.

The children were very surprised when the Angel left the Chalice and Host suspended in the air. Then he bent down and adored God, repeating the Angel's Prayer 3 times.

The Angel rose, took the Chalice and Host into his hands, and placed the Sacred Host in Lucia's mouth. He then gave the Chalice to Francisco and Jacinta saying.

"Take and drink—the Body and Blood of Jesus Christ horribly outraged by ungrateful men. Make reparation for their crimes."

The Angel's Prayer

Most Holy Trinity, Father, Son, and Holy Spirit, I adore You profoundly and offer You the most precious Body, and Blood, Soul and Divinity of Jesus Christ, present in all the tabernacles of the world, in reparation for all the outrages, sacrileges and indifference by which He is offended.

Through the infinite merits of the Most sacred Heart of Jesus and the Immaculate Heart of Mary, I beg of you the conversion of poor sinners.

? What is the Holy Eucharist?

Through a Priest and Holy Mass God changes bread and wine into the body and blood of Jesus and what was bread and wine is then called the Holy Eucharist, Holy Communion or the Blessed Sacrament.

The Angel came to the children three times to prepare them to receive a most important message from our Heavenly Mother.

What were some of the ways the Angel prepared them for the sacrament?

He taught them two new prayers that came from heaven the Par __ __ n Prayer and the An__ __ __ Prayer.

He was disappointed because the children were not Pr __ __ ing enough so he asked them to pray much more.

He taught them how important it was to S __ __ __ __ __ __ __ __ and how God was pleased with their sacrifices.

He brought them the Eu __ __ a __ __ __ t from Heaven.

The May Vision

Lucia and her two friends took their flock of sheep to the Cova da Iria, one of their favorite places to play. After a while, they began to get tired and Lucia said, **"This is such a beautiful day. Let's rest under this tree and say the Rosary."**

Then they saw something startling. Lucia said, **"Did you see a flash of lightning?"**

A beautiful Lady in sparkling white more brilliant than the sun appeared floating over a small holm oak tree. The children moved closer. The beautiful light from the lady sparkled and danced around them.

The Lady spoke so sweetly, **"Do not be afraid."**

Lucia replied, "**Where do you come from?**"

"I come from Heaven," said the Lady.

"I don't see anyone," Francisco said.

Lucia asked the Lady, **"Why can't Francisco see you?"**

"Tell him to say his Rosary and then he will see me."

Lucia turned to Francisco saying, **"The Lady says for you to pray your Rosary and then you will see her."**

Francisco took the Rosary from his pocket and began to pray the Hail Mary.

Suddenly, Francisco spoke out in an excited voice, **"I see her! I see her!"**

Lucia was so excited she asked the Lady, **"Do you come from heaven, and shall I go to heaven?"**

"Yes, you will," replied our Lady.

"And Jacinta?" Lucia asked.

"She will also."

Lucia then asked about Francisco. The Lady said, **"He will too but Francisco must pray many rosaries."**

Then the lady asked the children, **"Will you offer yourselves to God and bear all the sufferings that He sends you in reparation for all the sins that offend Him?"**

The children responded togeather, **"Yes, oh yes, we will!"**

Then the lady opened her hands and a stream of light came forth allowing them to see themselves in the outpouring love of God. The children fell to their knees, overwhelmed with the warmth and love that came from this glow. They prayed, **"Most Holy Trinity, I adore you. My God, my God, I love you in the Most Blessed Sacrament."**

As she disappeared into the distant sky, the beautiful Lady said, **"Say the Rosary every day to bring peace to the world."**

Troubles

As Jacinta, Lucia, and Francisco returned home, they agreed it would be better not to tell anyone about what they saw but little Jacinta was so excited; she could not keep the good news to herself. Before long, her whole family knew about the lovely Lady from Heaven.

When Lucia's mother heard what Jacinta said, she became very upset.

She said, "All this talk cannot be true, it must stop!"

Poor Jacinta felt very bad until Lucia whispered in her cousin's ear, "Don't worry. I'll get Francisco and we will all go to the well where we saw the Angel and we will pray."

When the three children got to the well Jacinta bravely said, "We must not be afraid of anything! Our dear Lady will help us, for she truly is our good friend."

They remembered that the Lady said that whenever there was something to do or a trial to suffer they should offer it to Jesus as a sacrifice. So they folded their hands and prayed, "O Jesus, it is for love of Thee and the conversion of sinners."

Prayer

O Jesus, it is for love of Thee and the conversion of sinners that we suffer trials.

This is an actual picture of the Fatima children praying.

Sometimes, the three children would pray even though playing would be more fun. They would give their lunches to poor children or their water to the sheep so they could offer their thirst to God as a sacrifice.

In the deepest, most hidden part of their souls, the children understood the great value of penance, and of making even little sacrifices out of love for God.

13.

The June Vision

On 13th day in June at the same hour, the children returned to the Cova. This time six other people joined them. The three little children recited the Rosary just as Our Lady asked them.

As they finished praying the Rosary, Lucia looked up and pointed to the east. "Look, see the light." Jacinta cried out with joy, "The Lady is here."

Lucia looked up at the Lady, "Please tell me what you want of me?"

"I want you to return here next month on the 13th and I want you to continue praying the Rosary as I taught you," replied the Lady.

Lucia asked her, "Will you please take us to heaven with you?"

The Lady answered, "Yes, I will take Jacinta and Francisco with me to heaven soon but you must remain here a little bit longer.

"Jesus wishes to make use of you to make me known and loved."

Once more, the Lady opened her hands and the children saw themselves immersed in God. At her right hand, they saw a heart surrounded by thorns. This was the Immaculate Heart of Mary.

Then she disappeared.

Lucia said, "Look! There she goes! There she goes! She is going back to Heaven."

Artwork by Joe DeVito

? What is Meant by the Immaculate Heart of Mary?

When we think of the Immaculate Heart of Mary, we think of Mary's life on earth, the wonderful joy she felt as Jesus's mother and the sorrow she felt when her Son suffered for us. We also think of Mary's love for all of us.

Think of how Mary's love for us can help us try to love God and all people as much she loves us.

Jesus   Mary   Father   Mother   Sister   Brother   Friends   Teacher

Pick one or more of the people above and finish the sentence to complete:

Some of the ways I can show my love for _____
                                                                          (PICK NAMES FROM ABOVE)

_____ are _____

_____

Difficult Days

The days following the Lady's visit in June were difficult. News of what the children saw spread rapidly and people asked them many questions.

Lucia's mother was scared and she also thought Lucia was making up stories. Many other people did not believe the children, they tried to get them to say they did not see the Lady.

Even though they suffered much and were scared, the children knew they had to keep telling the truth and offer their sufferings to God.

When you have been scared, what helped you feel better? Circle all that made you feel better or that you would want to do to make you feel better.

☐ Talk to your Mother or Father   ☐ Talk to your Friends

☐ Pray to God   ☐ Talk to your Priest

☐ Pray to Jesus   ☐ Talk to your Teacher

☐ Pray to Mary   ☐ Talk to your Grandparents

☐ Pray to a Saint   ☐ Talk to your Brother or Sister

Do you have another person you would talk to
or another way to help you feel better?

_____

_____

_____

_____

_____

_____

The July Vision

On July 13th the children prayed the Rosary while waiting for the beautiful Lady to return. A great crowd gathered at the Cova and just like the other times, only the children saw the mysterious light and the beautiful Lady!

Upon seeing the lady, Lucia asked, "Dear Lady won't you please tell us who you are? Jacinta, Francisco, and I think you are Jesus' Mother, but the villagers don't believe us. They think we are lying. Could you perform a miracle now so that they will believe?"

The Lady looked kindly at the children and said, "In October I will tell you who I am and I WILL perform a miracle at that time so all may believe."

Lucia asked Mary for a miracle so people would believe her. The miracle that took place in Fatima on October 13, 1917 was studied by the Church and was approved. We will learn more about the amazing Fatima miracle later in the story.

The Lady continued, "Sacrifice yourselves for sinners and pray the "Sacrifice Prayer" often, especially when you make a sacrifice.

? What is a Miracle?

When God changes what would normally happen to something wonderful we call it a miracle.

We can pray to God to perform a miracle. We can also ask Mary and the Saints to pray for a miracle to help us or to help someone else.

Sacrifice Prayer

O Jesus, this is for love of Thee, in reparation for the sins committed against the Immaculate Heart of Mary and for the conversion of poor sinners.'"

Say this prayer to allow any hardship, illness or pain you have to be offered as an Act of Reparation. How wonderful it is to be able to turn something that is bad into so much good by offering the pain and suffering as a sacrifice to God!

? What is an Act of Reparation?

An Act of Reparation is a sacrifice offered to God that repairs damage caused by sins of other people. Repairing damage makes our world a better place and helps save the souls of others.

Sacrament:
Sacrament of Reconciliation

The Sacrament of Reconciliation takes place when you make a good confession and find God's unconditional forgiveness for our sins against Him. We celebrate God's great mercy for us and we are called to forgive others.

The July Vision of Hell

The Lady then showed the three children something that she asked they keep secret. The children were given a special grace, a gift that was horrifying yet good for their souls and the world: they were allowed a vision of hell.

Our Lady spoke to the children. You have now seen hell where the souls of poor sinners go. But, if you do what I tell you, many souls will be saved and the world will become peaceful.

The Lady then asked the children to say a prayer we call the "Fatima Prayer" after each 10 Hail Mary's (decade) of the Rosary:

Lucia looked up at the Lady, saying, "She is rising to Heaven. Dear Lady, we will do as you ask."

Fatima Prayer

Oh my Jesus, forgive us our sins. Save us from the fires of Hell. Lead all souls to Heaven, especially those in most need of Your Mercy.

? What is Hell?

During our lives we choose to know and love God and we work hard to choose His will over our own. We are also called to know and love each other and forgive each other just as we ask for God's forgiveness. Hell is a place where people who willfully turn away from God go after they die. The greatest suffering for those in hell is that they will always be separated from God.

The August Vision

On August 13, 1917, as the children waited for the Lady to come, the leader of the government visited the children. He did not believe that they saw the beautiful Lady and he told them to stop lying and tell everyone that what they saw and heard did not happen.

Lucia, Jacinta and Francisco told him that they would be lying if they said what he wanted them to say. He got mad, threw them in prison and told them he would boil them in oil.

The three children knew the Lady and God did not want them to lie. That gave them the courage to tell the truth even though they were very afraid. When the government leader saw the children leading the prisoners in praying the Rosary, he finally gave up and took them back home.

What is the Glory Be Prayer?

How scary it must have been for the three young shepherd children to be in prison. They were fortunate that they knew how to pray the Rosary. The "Glory Be" is one of the prayers we learn so we can pray the Rosary.

Praying to God and asking for Mary's help brought them so much comfort that even the older prisoners saw their relief, joined them in prayer and felt so much better knowing that they were with God and God was with them.

The Glory Be Prayer

Glory be to the Father, the Son,
and the Holy Spirit;

as it was in the beginning,
is now, and ever shall be,

world without end.
Amen.

"The Glory Be" prayer is said before the "Our Father" prayer at each decade of the Rosary, during Holy Mass and whenever we feel like praying this prayer.

When we say this prayer, we show our love for the Blessed Trinity: One God in God the Father, God the Son (Jesus) and God the Holy Spirit.

When do we say the Glory Be Prayer while praying the Rosary?

_____

_____

_____

_____

The August Vision

A few days later the Lady appeared. She knew what had happened to the children and spoke kindly to them. She asked them to continue to pray the Rosary and to make sacrifices for poor sinners.

The Lady said sadly, "So many souls go to hell because they have no one to pray and make sacrifices for them."

Before leaving, the Lady told them that a Chapel should be built where she had appeared. The children then watched as she rose to heavens.

A small chapel was built as the Lady asked and many people visited to learn about the message of Fatima and to pray by the statue of Our Lady of Fatima. After a while so many people came that a large shrine was built where the Lady had appeared. We can visit this shrine today in Fatima, Portugal.

Our Lady of Fatima Statue at the Fatima Shrine

The September Vision

It was now the 13th of September and the children prayed the Rosary and waited for Our Lady to appear. But, they were not alone because 30,000 people joined them to learn about the Lady.

Lucia saw her first and she called out with excitement, "Our Lady is coming! Look above! I see Our Lady! Sweet Lady, what do you want of me?"

Our Lady again told Lucia how important it was to pray and to pray often. She said in her sweet, loving voice, "Continue to say your Rosary each day, my children. In October I will grant your request for a miracle so that everyone may believe. Our Lord will come and St. Joseph will appear with the Child Jesus to bless the world. God is pleased with your sacrifices."

Then the Lady went back to Heaven.

Do God and Mary think it is important to pray every day?

YES ☐   NO ☐

Is it important to pray the Rosary?

YES ☐   NO ☐

Is it important to make acts of reparation to repair the damage sin causes?

YES ☐   NO ☐

If you don't pray every day now would you like to start?

YES ☐   NO ☐

Would you like to learn how to pray the Rosary?

YES ☐   NO ☐

The October Vision

On October 13th in 1917, 70,000 people came to see the Miracle that the Lady promised. Lucia asked everyone to put down their umbrellas. Even though it was raining, all the people joined to pray the Rosary. At noon, a bright light suddenly flashed and the Lady appeared. Lucia was so excited.

Unable to wait any longer, Lucia eagerly asked, "Dear Lady, what do you want of me?"

The Lady smiled sweetly, and told the children she was Jesus's mother. She said, "I am the LADY OF THE ROSARY. I would like a Chapel built here in my honor. Continue to pray the Rosary every day."

As the Lady continued her eyes became sad. She said, "Men must change their lives and ask forgiveness for their sins. They must stop offending God who is already too much offended."

The Lady then opened her hands and a great ray of light extended from her hands into the sun.

Lucia cried out, "Look at the sun!"

The October Vision

The people immediately raised their eyes to the sky and everyone stared in amazement. The dark rain clouds disappeared and suddenly the sun came out.

Then the sun began doing very strange things. It looked as if it was dancing or spinning like a giant top. A most beautiful sight appeared. The sun began to shine beautiful rays of light on the entire countryside. It was like a tremendous fireworks display, but even more beautiful!

30.

A strange strong wind blew but the leaves on the trees did not move. In a few minutes the wind stopped and the people looked around and saw that the muddy ground suddenly became dry. Then they looked at each other in amazement because their wet and muddy clothes were now dry and even cleaner than when they had put them on.

Then the Holy Family appeared followed by Our Lady of the Rosary and beside her was the Child Jesus and St. Joseph too. Finally, Jesus appeared as a grown man and blessed all the people who saw the miracle.

With great joy, they all shouted, "A MIRACLE! A MIRACLE! GOD BE PRAISED!"

Yes, it was a miracle ...
the very miracle the Lady promised.

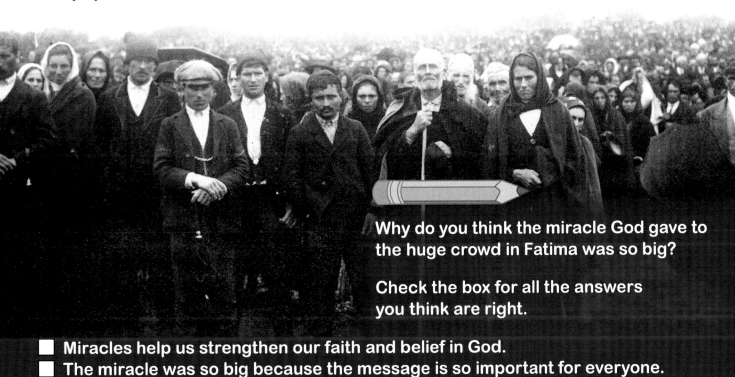

Why do you think the miracle God gave to the huge crowd in Fatima was so big?

Check the box for all the answers you think are right.

- [ ] Miracles help us strengthen our faith and belief in God.
- [ ] The miracle was so big because the message is so important for everyone.
- [ ] The people would not believe the children were telling the truth and the miracle helped the people believe them.
- [ ] God wants us to know that He loves us and will help us when we ask.

31.

Epilogue

Was this the end of the story? Oh, no the three shepherd children spent their days happily together fulfilling the wishes of Our Lady. They continued to take the sheep to the Cova to graze and they played, prayed and continued to make sacrifices to God.

The message of Fatima still lives on and must live on in all of us. We must live our lives as the message asks us to and spread the wonderful news to our family and friends.

In December 1918, a flu epidemic spread throughout the land. Many people died and soon Francisco became sick. Our Lady came to him and told him that she would soon take him to Heaven. Although he was very sick, Francisco went to church where he visited his Hidden Jesus, in the Eucharist. When he was too sick to go to Church, he asked Lucia to visit Jesus for him.

When he was sick, Francisco offered up his pain to God as a sacrifice. Our Lady came to visit him on April 4th in 1919 and she took Francisco to heaven.

Epilogue

Jacinta also became sick, even with all of her suffering, she never complained because she knew that she turned her bad pain into something good when she offered it to God. Our Lady came to visit Jacinta three times while she was sick. She told Jacinta that she would be taken to a hospital and that she would be all alone.

While in the hospital, Our Lady asked Jacinta if she would like to come to Heaven. Jacinta told her that she wanted to stay and suffer longer because she knew that by accepting her suffering and offering it to God she was saving many souls. Our Lady let her stay a while longer but then took her to Heaven on February 20, 1920.

Lucia missed her two cousins very much, but she knew that someday they would be together in heaven. She continued to do what Our Lady asked. The small Chapel the townspeople built in Fatima where Our Lady appeared has now become a large shrine.

Millions of people go there to pray, receive Our Lord in the Eucharist and receive blessings. Through Our Lady's words, we are reminded to choose to do what God wants us to do instead of what we want to do, to pray often and to offer sacrifices to God. Sister Lucia lived a very long time to help us learn, live and spread this wonderful message from Heaven.

Our Blessed Mother took Sister Lucia to Heaven on a special day, February 13, 2005.

This is the true story of the three little shepherd children of Fatima, Portugal.

But the story isn't over yet.

Many more people need to learn the message, to pray and to make sacrifices. As you share this book and the wonderful animated film, "The Day the Sun Danced, The True Story of Fatima," with your family and friends you help bring people closer to God and to peace.

How Do We Pray From Our Heart?

Mary, Our Heavenly Mother wants us to sacrifice and pray the Rosary often. Another prayer we learn to pray the Rosary is the Our Father. We also pray this prayer at Holy Mass. We can pray the Our Father any time we want to pray to God. We can also pray to God just by talking to him.

The Our Father prayer is sometimes called The Lord's Prayer. Like the Hail Mary Prayer, the Our Father comes from the Bible. Pay close attention to the meaning of the words as you read the prayer.

Prayers that come from Heaven can be very powerful if we understand them and say them from our heart.

Our Father Prayer

Our Father, who art in heaven,
hallowed be thy name; thy kingdom come;
thy will be done on earth as it is in heaven.
Give us this day our daily bread;
and forgive us our trespasses
as we forgive those who trespass
against us; and lead us not into
temptation, but deliver us
from evil.

Amen.

As we say this prayer we are saying that we want God's will to be done. Sometimes it is hard for us to choose to do what God wants us to do, especially if we want to do something else.

What are some of the reasons it is so important to choose to do God's will rather than our own? Try to answer without help and then ask for help from your religious teacher, parents, grandparents or priest.

1._____

2._____

3._____

What Does It Mean to Trespass?

When we choose to do something that God would not want us to do it is interfering with God's will or trespassing on His will.

In the Our Father prayer we ask God to forgive us our trespasses as we forgive others who trespass against us.

Why is so important for us to forgive others even when we don't want to, or they don't forgive us or when they treat us badly? Again, think about it and answer on your own and then ask for help.

_____

_____

_____

_____

_____

Forgiving someone is different than allowing someone to bully or treat you badly. Although we must forgive, we shouldn't let others treat us badly. If someone will not stop treating you badly, tell your teacher, parents, grandparents, or priest so that they can help you.

Prayer

We begin the Rosary by making the sign of the cross and saying:

"In the name of the Father, and of the Son and of the Holy Spirit. Amen."

The first prayer of the Rosary is the Apostles Creed. This prayer is also said during Holy Mass. This is a wonderful prayer that talks about many of the most important things we believe in as Catholics. Read it very carefully so you can understand what it means. Some parts may be hard to understand, ask for help from your religious teacher, parents, grandparents, or a priest.

The Apostles' Creed

I believe in God, the Father almighty, Creator of heaven and earth,
and in Jesus Christ, His only Son, our Lord,
who was conceived by the Holy Spirit, born of the Virgin Mary,
suffered under Pontius Pilate, was crucified, died and was buried;
He descended into hell; on the third day He rose again from the dead;
He ascended into heaven,
and is seated at the right hand of God the Father Almighty;
from there He will come to judge the living and the dead.
I believe in the Holy Spirit, the Holy Catholic Church,
the Communion of Saints, the forgiveness of sins,
the resurrection of the body,
and life everlasting.
Amen.

Hail, Holy Queen

Hail, Holy Queen, Mother of Mercy, our life,
our sweetness, and our hope. To thee do we cry, poor
banished children of Eve. To thee do we send up our sighs
mourning and weeping in this valley of tears. Turn then, most
gracious advocate, thine eyes of mercy toward us, and after
this our exile show us the blessed fruit of thy womb, Jesus.
O clement, O loving, O sweet Virgin Mary.
(Verse) Pray for us, O Holy Mother of God.
(Response) That we may be made
worthy of the promises of
Christ.

Rosary Prayer

(Verse) Let us pray,
(Response) O God, whose only begotten Son, by His life, death, and
resurrection, has purchased for us the rewards of eternal salvation.
Grant, we beseech Thee, that while meditating on these mysteries
of the most Holy Rosary of the Blessed Virgin Mary, that we
may both imitate what they contain and obtain what they
promise, through Christ our Lord. Amen.
Most Sacred Heart of Jesus,
have mercy on us.
Immaculate Heart of Mary,
pray for us.

The Mysteries of the Rosary

When praying the Rosary we think about Jesus's life. Each mystery helps us think about what the Bible teaches us about Jesus. Cadets 4 Mary will receive more information about each mystery on the Cadet website and by email. Your religious teacher can also provide more information about each mystery.

The Five Joyful Mysteries
are traditionally prayed on the Mondays, Saturdays, and Sundays of Advent:

1. The Annunciation
2. The Visitation
3. The Nativity
4. The Presentation in the Temple
5. The Finding in the Temple

The Five Glorious Mysteries
are traditionally prayed on the Wednesday and Sundays outside of Lent and Advent:

1. The Resurrection
2. The Ascension
3. The Descent of the Holy Spirit
4. The Assumption
5. The Coronation of Mary

The Five Sorrowful Mysteries
are traditionally prayed on the Tuesday, Friday, and Sundays of Lent:

1. The Agony in the Garden
2. The Scourging at the Pillar
3. The Crowning with Thorns
4. The Carrying of the Cross
5. The Crucifixion and Death

The Five Luminous Mysteries
are traditionally prayed on Thursdays:

1. The Baptism of Christ in the Jordan
2. The Wedding Feast at Cana
3. Jesus' Proclamation of the Coming of the Kingdom of God
4. The Transfiguration
5. The Institution of the Eucharist

How to Pray the Rosary

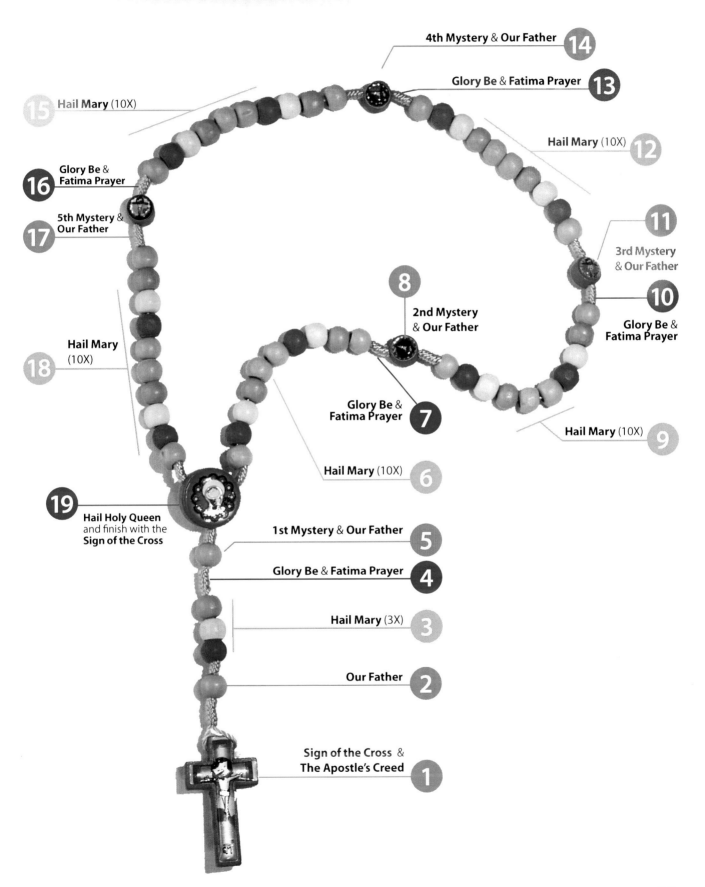

4th Mystery & **Our Father** — 14

Glory Be & **Fatima Prayer** — 13

15 — **Hail Mary** (10X)

Hail Mary (10X) — 12

16 — **Glory Be** & **Fatima Prayer**

17 — **5th Mystery** & **Our Father**

11 — **3rd Mystery** & **Our Father**

8 — **2nd Mystery** & **Our Father**

10 — **Glory Be** & **Fatima Prayer**

18 — **Hail Mary** (10X)

Glory Be & **Fatima Prayer** — 7

Hail Mary (10X) — 9

Hail Mary (10X) — 6

19 — **Hail Holy Queen** and finish with the **Sign of the Cross**

1st Mystery & **Our Father** — 5

Glory Be & **Fatima Prayer** — 4

Hail Mary (3X) — 3

Our Father — 2

Sign of the Cross & **The Apostle's Creed** — 1

Cadets 4 Mary Membership

Become a Cadet 4 Mary

and join friends from around the world who are learning and living the powerful message of Our Lady of Fatima.

Cadet Goals

The three main goals of Fatima Family Apostolate's **Cadet's 4 Mary** program are to live and Spread Our Lady's Message of Hope, a plan for holiness given to the children of Fatima. To become a Cadet, one must sign the Cadet Pledge and strive to live it. This pledge does not bind under sin. Those who pledge promise the Blessed Mother they will strive to do what she asked at Fatima.

Cadets 4 Mary Membership Pledge

Dear Heavenly Mother, I wish to do everything you asked when you appeared to the three children in Fatima. To help repair the damage caused by my sins and save the souls of others I promise I will to strive to:

1. Pray every day, especially the Rosary.
2. Do God's will when tempted to do something He would not want me to do.
3. Offer Sacrifices to God as Our Lady of Fatima asked of us.
4. Practice a life of holiness and forgiveness.

Sign _____   Sign _____

Sign _____   Sign _____

Sign _____   Sign _____

This is a Spiritual Pledge to strive to live a faith centered life of holiness.
It is not a vow and does not bind under sin.

After you sign the Cadets 4 Mary Pledge you automatically join thousands of others over many generation who have signed a Cadet Pledge.
You are also eligible to receive:

Cadet 4 Mary
Membership Card

Cadet 4 Mary
Membership Certificate

Your Name Here

- Your Certificate of Membership, suitable for framing
- Your Membership Card
- The ability to connect with members worldwide
- Additional cadet information

To receive the additional member benefits and much more, visit the official Cadets 4 Mary website, or write to the Fatima Family Apostolate USA Center:

Fatima Family Apostolate International
PO Box 269
Hanceville, AL 35077

www.Cadets4Mary.org

(800) 213-5541

Fr. Fox's
Fatima Family Apostolate International

Almost thirty years ago, the Vatican encouraged Father Robert J. Fox, who was widely known as "The Fatima Priest," to form the Fatima Family Apostolate. The mission of the Apostolate is to promote the sanctification of family life and the authentic message of Fatima. We are a teaching apostolate with prayer groups all around the world.

Father Fox was a prolific author who is widely acclaimed as the US Fatima expert. He has written over fifty books that reflect his deep understanding of the Catholic faith. His timeless work is available from the Fatima Family Apostolate and through Catholic book and gift stores.

The Fatima Family Apostolate also publishes the spiritually enriching and beautiful magazine, *The Immaculate Heart Messenger.*

The Apostolate International Center welcomes all to visit our beautiful outdoor shrines, chapel and gift shop. We are located in Hanceville, Alabama just 12 miles from the Shrine of the Most Blessed Sacrament, home of EWTN's Mother Angelica and the Poor Clare Nuns.

To learn more, please call 1-800-213-5541 or visit us online at www.fatimafamily.org.

Like us on Facebook and Twitter

CCC exists to produce and distribute engaging, high-quality entertainment with authentic family values. We use media to communicate faith-filled fun, wherein people can discover stories of real heroes possessing courage, love and truth. Presenting the goodness of man and the beauty of life, CCC of America has emerged with a better alternative – entertainment you can believe in.

CCC of America "Saints and Heroes" children animated series of 11 titles is well known and loved by families around the globe. These stories live in the hearts of many generations and through them they have discovered true stories of real heroes possessing courage, love and upholding truth. Presenting the goodness and authentic virtues over the years our tag line had truly represented the mission of these films, to provide families entertainment they can truly believe in.

Breaking through in the field of animation, in 1988 CCC produced their first animated film, The Day the Sun Danced: The True Story of Fatima. A true privilage to work with Fr. Robert Fox with extensive knowledge and passion to spread the message of Fatima. CCC also worked closely with Fatima Apostolates in the US and Portugal.

New titles continued to be added in the years that followed, creating the now classic collection of 11 Saints & Heroes animated films series.

THE DAY THE SUN DANCED
The True Story Of Fatima

is the inspiring true story of Lucia, Francisco and Jacinta, whose great faith and courage brought the message of Our Lady of Fatima for the entire world from a tiny village in Fatima, Portugal.

A Fatima Book
for Each Child

If you believe, as we do,

...that the world is in need of Our Lady of Fatima's Message of Hope, please consider supporting the "A Fatima Book for Each Child Program." The Program's mission is to provide this book, The Miracle of the Dancing Sun at Fatima, Messages from Mary, to parishes and schools to use in their classrooms.

In future printings, one full page will be reserved in this book to express our gratitude for those who support the "Fatima Book for Each Child Program." If you can help large groups of children, please contact us to learn how to reserve a full or a half page.